W9-BYQ-470

J996 WB

EARLY PEOPLES

THE POLYNESIANS

WORLD
BOOK

World Book
a Scott Fetzer company
Chicago
www.worldbookonline.com

World Book, Inc.
233 N. Michigan Avenue
Chicago, IL 60601
U.S.A.

For information about other World Book publications, visit our
Web site at http://www.worldbookonline.com or call
1-800-WORLDBK (967-5325).
For information about sales to schools and libraries, call
1-800-975-3250 (United States), or 1-800-837-5365 (Canada).

Library of Congress Cataloging-in-Publication Data

The Polynesians.
    p. cm. -- (Early peoples)
  Includes index.
  Summary: "A discussion of the early Polynesians, including
who they were, where they lived, the rise of civilization, social
structure, religion, art and architecture, science and technology,
daily life, entertainment and sports, and fall of civilization.
Features include timelines, fact boxes, glossary, list of
recommended reading and web sites"--Provided by publisher.
  ISBN 978-0-7166-2140-9
  1. Polynesians--Juvenile literature. I. World Book, Inc.
GN670.P57 2009
305.8994--dc22
                                        2008032225

Printed in China by Leo Paper Products Ltd.,
Heshan, Guangdong
2nd printing June 2010

STAFF

TABLE OF CONTENTS

Glossary There is a glossary on pages 60-61. Terms defined in the glossary are in type **that looks like this** on their first appearance on any spread (two facing pages).

Additional Resources Books for further reading and recommended Web sites are listed on page 62. Because of the nature of the Internet, some Web site addresses may have changed since publication. The publisher has no responsibility for any such changes or for the content of cited sources.

WHO WERE THE POLYNESIANS?

The Polynesians *(POL uh NEE zhuhnz)* are a group of peoples who settled—and still live on—islands in the central Pacific Ocean. The Hawaiians, Samoans, Tahitians, and Tongans, as well as the Maori *(MAH oh ree* or *MOW ree)* of New Zealand, are the largest groups of Polynesian peoples.

The Polynesians adapted well to life in a world dominated by the ocean. Skillful sailors and boatbuilders, the Polynesians were the first people known to make long ocean voyages. They discovered and settled almost every island in the central Pacific hundreds of years before Europeans explored the area.

The Polynesians shared similar religious beliefs, social customs, and languages. All Polynesians believed in **mana** *(MAH nah)* and **taboo** *(tuh BOO* or *ta BOO)*. Mana was the most important Polynesian religious belief. It was a **supernatural** *(SOO puhr NACH uhr uhl)* force connected to gods, spirits, powerful individuals, and special objects. Taboo was the basis of law and behavior in Polynesia. Taboo prohibited certain actions, activities, and foods because they were sacred, dangerous, or unclean. The Polynesians worshiped many gods and spirits.

▼ Carved figures of gods, called **tikis** *(TEE keez)*, stand guard at Pu'uhonua o Honaunau National Historic Park in Hawaii. Polynesians believed that such figures contained mana, or spiritual power.

A Class-Conscious People

Class and rank mattered greatly to the Polynesians. The Polynesians were divided into **clans**. Everyone born to a clan was believed to share a common ancestor. People were ranked depending on how closely related they were to the common ancestor. The man most closely related was the clan chief. People were divided into classes by rank and occupation. There were three main classes: chiefs, experts (priests and craftspeople), and commoners (farmers and fishers). Marriage between people of different classes was forbidden. Warfare between chiefs was common.

The Polynesians used simple tools made of stone, wood, plant fibers, bone, and shells. Their greatest technological achievement was their ocean-going canoes.

▲ Coral reefs surround the island of Tahiti in French Polynesia. This mountainous island was formed by two long-extinct volcanoes.

Many Languages

Polynesians speak about 30 different languages, but these languages have many words in common. Even if they come from islands that are thousands of miles apart, Polynesians can speak to and understand one another. About 1 million people speak Polynesian languages today. Many other people consider themselves to be Polynesian but now speak English or French as their main language. Modern Polynesians are mostly Christians, and belief in mana, taboo, and the traditional gods has diminished. Polynesian art still flourishes, and the Polynesian sport of surfing is popular around the world.

WHAT'S IN A NAME?
The name *Polynesia* comes from Greek words meaning *many islands.* European explorers gave this name to the central Pacific because of its thousands of small islands.

HOW DO WE KNOW ABOUT POLYNESIAN HISTORY?

◀ A boat-shaped ring of stones once formed the foundation of a house on Easter Island. Archaeologists believe the holes in the stones are slots that held roof timbers and that the stone paved area was a patio. Several of the giant **moai** *(MOH eye)* statues for which the island is famous appear in the background.

The earliest written accounts of the Polynesians were by European explorers and **missionaries** *(MIHSH uh nehr eez)*. These accounts make exciting reading. They can be misleading, however, because these visitors did not understand the Polynesians' way of life and missionaries often did not approve of the Polynesians' religious beliefs.

Polynesians did not use writing to record their history before modern times. Stories and legends about the past were passed down by word of mouth from one generation to the next. Polynesians learned how to write after they made contact with Europeans. They then wrote their own accounts of their peoples' customs and history.

A major source of knowledge about early Polynesian history comes from the science of **archaeology** *(AHR kee OL uh jee)*. Archaeology is the scientific study of the remains left by people who lived in the past. These remains include buildings, tools, and burial sites. **Archaeologists** even study garbage because it can tell them what kinds of food people ate. Archaeologists discover these remains by **excavating** sites where people once lived and worked.

DAVID MALO

David Malo (1793-1853) was one of the first Hawaiians to learn reading and writing from Christian missionaries. Although he became a Christian minister, Malo did not forget the stories about his people's history and beliefs that he had heard as a child at the court of King Kamehameha *(kuh MAY hah MAY hah)*. A great storyteller, Malo wrote a popular book about Hawaiian history in 1839. The book was the first permanent record of the history of the Hawaiian people.

▲ An archaeologist carefully measures the ruins of a prehistoric house on Easter Island. Archaeological excavations have revealed important information about the way early Polynesians lived.

The most common Polynesian **artifacts** found by archaeologists are tools made of shell, bone, and stone. Ruins of stone forts and temples have been discovered on some islands, including Hawaii. The most impressive archaeological discoveries in Polynesia are the giant carved-stone heads on Easter Island.

Archaeologists have worked with Polynesian sailors to build and sail traditional Polynesian boats. Learning these skills helps archaeologists understand how the Polynesians were able to explore such a vast area of the ocean.

On some remote islands, Polynesians were able to live according to their traditional ways well into the 1900's. **Anthropologists** *(AN thruh POL uh jihstz)*, scientists who study human cultures, studied these Polynesians. They talked to them about their lives and made records of their customs and beliefs.

In the Genes

All people carry evidence about their ancestors in their **DNA**. DNA is the substance that **genes** *(jeenz)* are made of. Genes are the parts of a cell that determine which characteristics a living thing inherits from its parents. Scientists can study genes to trace a person's ancestry back for hundreds or thousands of years. By studying the genes of living Polynesians, scientists have learned where their ancestors originally came from.

ORIGINS OF THE POLYNESIANS

The Polynesians are descendants of the Lapita *(lah PEE tuh)* people who lived on the Solomon Islands in the western Pacific Ocean.

The Polynesians are an **Austronesian** *(AWS troh NEE zhuhn)* people. The first Austronesians are thought to have lived on the island of Taiwan, off the coast of China. About 5,000 years ago, Austronesians began to leave Taiwan and settle on the Philippine Islands. From there, they spread through the islands of Southeast Asia and even across the Indian Ocean to Madagascar.

About 4,000 years ago, Austronesians settled on the Solomon Islands and the Bismarck **Archipelago** *(AHR kuh PEHL uh goh)*, a group of islands northeast of the island of New Guinea. The Austronesians mixed with earlier settlers from New Guinea and combined to form a new culture that **archaeologists** call the Lapita Culture. The Lapita people always settled close to the sea. They grew crops, bred pigs and chickens, and fished for food. They cooked and stored food in beautifully decorated clay pots.

▼ The Polynesians trace their ancestry to the Lapita people, Austronesians originally from Taiwan who settled in the Solomon Islands and Bismarck Archipelago and mixed with people from New Guinea. Over time, the Lapita **migrated** to a number of nearby islands, including Fiji, Samoa, and Tonga.

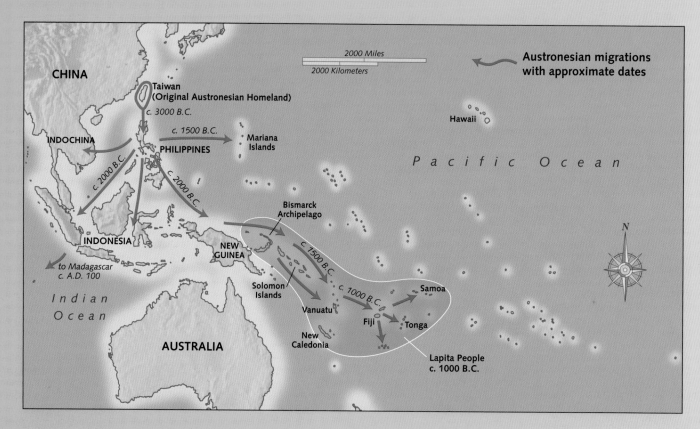

▲ Painted ceremonial masks from New Guinea were decorated with shells and feathers. Austronesians believed such masks enabled their wearers to communicate with the **supernatural** world.

The islands of Southeast Asia are close together. The Austronesians who settled in the Solomon Islands were able to get there by making many short voyages, hopping from one island to another. They never needed to sail far from land.

Into the Pacific

The Lapita people were not afraid to sail out of sight of land. About 3,500 years ago, they took a great step into the unknown, sailing east in search of new islands in the vast Pacific Ocean. By 3,000 years ago, the Lapita people had settled on the islands that became known as Fiji, New Caledonia, Samoa, Tonga, and Vanuatu. The Lapita people who settled on Fiji, Samoa, and Tonga were the ancestors of all of the Polynesians. The Polynesian culture and language developed on those islands from 500 B.C. to 300 B.C. Fiji is not now considered to be part of Polynesia because the Polynesians who lived there were later joined by other peoples.

The Lapita people must have been able to build sturdy sailing boats to travel so far. Archaeologists have not yet discovered the remains of any of their boats, however.

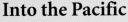

MEET THE AUSTRONESIANS

Austronesians form the majority of the populations of the countries of Indonesia, Madagascar, Malaysia, and the Philippines, as well as Polynesia. There are also Austronesian minorities living in Cambodia, Laos, Taiwan, and Vietnam. Altogether, there are over 200 million Austronesians today.

THE POLYNESIANS SETTLE THE PACIFIC ISLANDS

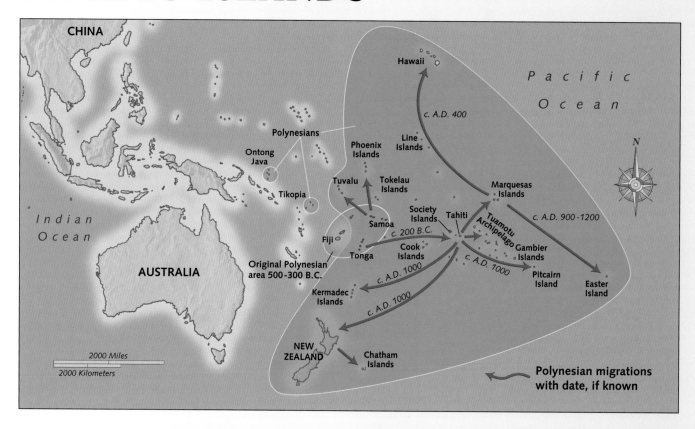

Polynesians from Tonga discovered and settled what is now Tahiti in the Society Islands about 2,200 years ago. These islands became the base from which the Polynesians spread out north, east, and southwest to settle islands in the rest of the central Pacific Ocean.

Not long after they settled in Tahiti, Polynesians began to settle in the Tuamotu (*TOO uh MOH too*) **Archipelago** and the Marquesas (*mahr KAY suhz*) Islands. These groups contain thousands of islands, and it took hundreds of years before every habitable island was settled. Sometime around A.D. 400, Polynesians from the Marquesas Islands discovered and began to settle the Hawaiian Islands, more than 2,000 miles (3,200 kilometers) to the north. The tiny

▲ From Tahiti in the Society Islands, Polynesians traveling in canoes explored and settled islands across a vast region of the central Pacific Ocean.

POLYNESIANS IN SOUTH AMERICA

Some scientists believe that chicken bones discovered at an Inca settlement in Chile prove that Polynesians reached South America. **Archaeologists** had believed that Spanish conquerors carried the first chickens to America, but the bones, found in 2007, were dated to the late 1300's, before the Spaniards arrived. The scientists believe that the **DNA** from the bones show that the chickens belonged to a breed kept by the Polynesians. Other scientists dispute the finding.

Line Islands are about halfway between the Marquesas and Hawaii. Ruins on these islands show that Polynesians lived on them for a time. When the first Europeans visited the Line Islands in 1777, however, they were uninhabited.

Polynesians from the Marquesas Islands settled Easter Island sometime between A.D. 900 and 1200. This island was even more remote than Hawaii. Pitcairn Island, halfway between Tahiti and Easter Island, was settled by Polynesians about 1,000 years ago.

New Zealand was the greatest discovery made by sailors from Tahiti. According to legend, about 1,000 years ago, a fisherman named Kupe *(koo peh)* discovered the islands of New Zealand by accident when chasing a giant octopus that had stolen his bait. The Polynesians who settled in New Zealand became known as the Maori. Scientists have evidence that some Polynesians sailed as far as South America, but it is unknown if they ever returned to Polynesia.

Overcrowded Lands

The Polynesians were skillful seafarers. However, there must have been many times when explorers set out and never returned because they ran out of food and water before discovering land or because they were shipwrecked or drowned. Why did they take the risk? Most of the Polynesian islands are small and soon would have become overcrowded. This forced people to look for new places to live. In addition, the Polynesians were a warlike people. Chiefs often fought one another for power. Experts think that some victors may have forced the losers to leave their home island and find a new island to live on.

▼ Moorea, in French Polynesia's Society Islands, was first settled by Polynesians around 2,200 years ago. Moorea is a mountainous island formed from an extinct volcano, with fertile soils and ample rainfall. Coral reefs around the coast are rich in fish.

ADAPTING TO THE PACIFIC ENVIRONMENT

The Pacific Islands have been compared to paradise. Their sandy beaches lined with palm trees and their warm, clear water make them great places to go for a vacation, but they can be tough places on which to live permanently. The Pacific Islands had few native food plants. The Polynesians were able to settle on the islands only because they brought crops and farm animals with them.

There are two types of islands in Polynesia, high islands and low islands. The high islands are mostly volcanic islands, created when volcanoes erupt from the sea floor. They gradually become taller and grow above the ocean surface. Samoa, Tonga, and the islands of Hawaii are all volcanic islands. Smoke rising from erupting volcanoes may have helped Polynesian explorers locate undiscovered islands.

The low islands are often coral reefs, which are formed by the skeletons of millions of tiny sea animals called coral. **Atolls** *(AT olz)* are the most common kind of coral island. Atolls are circular rings of coral that rise only a few feet above the sea. These islands form on the tops of ancient extinct volcanoes that have sunk back below the level of the sea. Atolls enclose lagoons *(luh GOONZ)*, or areas of shallow calm water that are completely or almost completely separated from the open sea.

The mountainous volcanic islands have the best environments. The mountains cause rain clouds to form, so there are plentiful supplies

▲ Molten lava pours from Kilauea *(KEE low AY ah)* volcano on Hawaii, the largest island in the Hawaiian Islands chain. Hawaiians believed the volcano was the home of Pele *(PAY lay)*, the volcano goddess.

of drinking water. Weather breaks down the volcanic rocks to soils that are highly fertile. Coral reefs that form around the coasts of these islands are good places to fish.

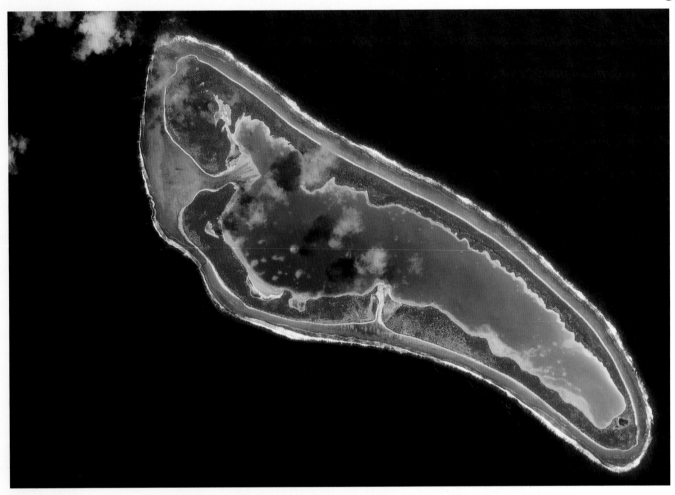

▲ Many Polynesian islands are atolls, roughly circular islands composed of the skeletons of tiny sea animals called corals. Atolls, which rise only a few feet above the sea, usually enclose a sheltered lagoon of shallow water.

A Tough Life

Life on coral islands is much harder. Because they are so low, coral islands often have little rainfall, so drinking water can be scarce. During severe storms, the sea can flood coral islands. The soil that forms on top of the coral is thin and infertile. The people who lived on coral islands depended much more on fishing for food than those who lived on volcanic islands.

The Polynesians found New Zealand an especially difficult place to settle. New Zealand has two main islands, both long and mountainous. The islands have fertile soil, good rainfall, and a cool climate. Unfortunately, most of the Polynesians' crops needed a warm, tropical climate to grow. New Zealand's Maori developed a way life different from that of other Polynesians. They hunted seals, whales, and giant ostrich-like birds called moas *(MOH uhz)*.

RATS

Polynesians took live rats on their voyages, either as stowaways or to eat. When Polynesians landed on new islands, rats escaped, bred quickly, and soon threatened native animals and plants. Dozens of species of birds that nested on the ground became extinct because rats ate their eggs. Some plants became extinct because rats ate their seeds.

CLANS AND CHIEFDOMS

◀ A French Polynesian chief wears a traditional headdress and cape of bird feathers with decorations of shark's teeth and iridescent mother-of-pearl from seashells. Such garments are believed to possess mana, or sacred power.

Polynesian society was divided into **clans** and chiefdoms. The basic unit was the clan, which was based on family ties. All members of a clan were related by birth—descended from a common ancestor—or by marriage.

Clan members were ranked according to how closely they were related to the clan's common ancestor. The clan chief was usually the man who was most closely related. Next in status was the chief's eldest son, who became chief after his father's death. Daughters had a lower status than sons. In Hawaii, Tahiti, and Tonga, women could become chiefs if there were no eligible men.

As the population increased, clans often split up to form new clans, each with its own territory and chief. Clans were ranked according to how closely related they were to the most powerful chief and his clan. Ancestry was so important for a person's status that people with an expert knowledge of a clan's ancestors were highly respected.

The power of chiefs varied considerably. On coral **atolls** with small populations, such as Tokelau *(TOH kuh lah oo)*, chiefs worked for a living like everyone else. The whole community met to make important decisions. Apart from the chiefs and a small number of priests, there were no social classes.

Social Classes

On islands with larger populations, such as Samoa, social classes developed. The main classes were chiefs, experts, and commoners. Experts included priests and craftspeople, such as boatbuilders. Most people were commoners. They lived by farming or fishing. The specialists and the commoners paid taxes to the chiefs in the form of food and craft products. They also performed labor for the chiefs. Some of the taxes were returned to the people at feasts and gift-giving ceremonies.

Chiefs were believed to possess a sacred power called **mana**, which came from the gods. Chiefs had to use their mana to benefit their people. If harvests were good or there was victory in war, people would be satisfied with their chief. Defeat in war or a poor harvest damaged a chief's authority because it was a sign that his mana was weak. Around the time of contact with Europeans, Tahiti, Tonga, and the Hawaiian Islands came to be ruled by kings. These **monarchies** *(MON uhr keez)* were founded by chiefs who conquered all the other chiefs on the islands in order to become king.

SYMBOLS OF POWER

Hawaiian chiefs wore helmets and cloaks made of bird feathers as a sign of their mana. The cape of the Hawaiian Chief Kiwala'o (above) is now part of a display at the Bishop Museum in Honolulu, Hawaii. Kiwala'o died in battle in 1782. To make a cloak, thousands of feathers were needed from the red 'I'iwi *(ee EE vee)* and yellow 'o'o birds. Bird catchers trapped the birds alive and released them after removing only one or two feathers from each. This ensured future supplies of feathers.

WARFARE

A fierce-looking head of the Hawaiian war god Ku is made of red feathers with mother-of-pearl eyes and dog's teeth. The worship of Ku included human sacrifice.

War was common in Polynesia. Wars were fought mainly to capture victims for human sacrifice and to seize farmland from neighboring chiefdoms. Victory in war increased a chief's status. By killing his enemies, he could take their **mana**. Success in battle was a way for commoners to increase their status, too. In Tonga, a commoner who took 10 enemy heads was given a land grant.

Battles were fought on land and also at sea between fleets of war canoes. Polynesian armies could be very large. In 1774, the British explorer James Cook (1728-1779) watched the war fleet of Tahiti set out to raid the nearby island of Moorea. He counted 330 canoes carrying about 8,000 warriors.

Chiefs believed that it was important to have the support of the gods in wartime. When the Hawaiian Chief Keoua (*KAY oh wah*) lost one-third of his army in a volcanic eruption, many people believed it was a sign that the volcano goddess Pele supported his enemy Kamehameha. As a result, many of Chief Keoua's supporters changed sides.

Fighting the Battle

Before a battle, warriors rubbed their skin with vegetable oil. This made their skin slippery so that enemy warriors could not grab hold of them. Warriors had no protection in battle—they did not use armor or shields. **Taboos** regulated the conduct of warfare. A raiding party halted before attacking a village and issued a formal challenge to its inhabitants to come out and fight. Sometimes both sides would work together to clear a battlefield of shrubs and trees to make fighting easier. Warriors only fought other warriors of equal rank.

Prisoners of war were not treated well. The lucky ones were enslaved. Most were tortured and sacrificed to the gods. Polynesians did not eat people for food, but sometimes parts of a dead enemy warrior were eaten as a final insult or to take the warrior's mana.

▲ The walls and tower of a ruined fortress is 1 of about 15 such fortifications on Rapa Island in French Polynesia. Scientists believe the forts indicate that the people of the island fought frequently, most likely over farmland and other natural resources.

Weapons with a Bite

Shark's teeth gave many Polynesian weapons a sharp saw-like edge that could inflict deadly wounds. Some spears had rows of shark's teeth fastened to the ends. Others had stone points or sharp wooden points that had been hardened in a fire. Longer spears were used for stabbing; shorter ones were thrown like javelins. Hawaiian warriors threw wooden axes with blades lined with shark's teeth at their enemies' legs.

TAHITIAN WAR CHANT

War is growth to the land
Establishment of great men
Spreading out of people
Take the war weapons
Dig the holes
War is fertile soil
Soil that will produce seeds
Soil that will be covered in green plants
Soil for priests
Soil for temples
Soil that changes rulers

MANA AND TABOO

Mana was the most important Polynesian religious belief. Mana is a **supernatural** force possessed by gods, people, and such special objects as canoes and tools. Mana was not shared equally among the people. The gods gave more mana to chiefs than to commoners.

A chief could increase his mana by sacrificing defeated enemies to the gods or by owning remarkable objects, such as a feather cloak. Mana was protected by **purification** (cleansing) ceremonies. Warriors preparing for war and sailors preparing for a dangerous voyage purified themselves by living apart from other people for a time. They avoided women and ate only special foods.

▲ Fish **petroglyphs** found on Easter Island may have been used to remind people that the animals were taboo at certain times. Fish, a major food source, became taboo during their breeding season and could not, therefore, be caught, protecting fish stocks from overfishing.

No Touching

The Polynesians did not have law codes and law courts. Instead, they had **taboos**. Taboos were **ritual** restrictions that forbade some activities because they were considered unclean or unsafe. People who broke a taboo were thought to be cursed. They might fall ill, have bad luck when fishing, or lose a close relative. Breaking a taboo could also stop the flow of mana from the gods, which would be bad for everyone. Because they received the most mana, chiefs had many taboos surrounding them. It was taboo for commoners to talk to a chief or to touch his head because this would make him impure and unworthy to receive mana. In many Polynesian societies, people who broke these taboos could be executed.

PLACE OF REFUGE

Taboo breakers in Hawaii were spared the death penalty if they escaped to a *pu'uhonua (poo oo hoh NOO ah)*, or place of **refuge**, such as the site at the Pu'uhonua o Honaunau National Historical Park (below). Refuges were built near the shore and the homes of chiefs. Taboo breakers risked being killed by the chief or his warriors if they tried to enter the refuge by land. Swimming along the coast to the refuge carried a risk of drowning or shark attack. Priests performed ceremonies in the refuge to purify taboo breakers, so that they could re-enter society. Defeated warriors fleeing from battle could also find safety in refuges.

Sacred objects and places, such as temples, were taboo because they contained the powerful mana of a god. It was not safe for a commoner with little mana to enter such places. Only people with strong mana, such as chiefs and priests, could enter without risking harm to themselves.

Polynesians used taboos to conserve resources. It was taboo to walk in the forest, pick fruit, or go fishing at certain times of year. Taboos governed all the important events in life, such as birth, marriage and death, and even such everyday matters as diet. In much of Polynesia, for example, it was taboo for men and women to eat together.

GODS AND MYTHS

THE GODS OF HAWAII

The four main Hawaiian gods were Kane *(KAH nay)*, the sky god; Ku *(koo)*, the war god; Lono *(LOH noh)*, the god of farming; and Kanaloa *(kah nah LOH wah)*, the sea god. The dozens of lesser gods included Pele, the volcano goddess; Kamapua'a *(KAH mah poo ah ah)*, the rain god; and Papa *(PAH pah)*, the nature goddess. Maui the trickster was a very popular god. He changed time, made islands, and gave human beings the secret of fire.

◀ Stone ancestor figures on Tahiti in French Polynesia. Polynesians believed they could communicate with their ancestors through these statues.

The Polynesians worshiped many gods. Some gods were widely known but were worshiped under slightly different names in different places. Other gods belonged to just one group of islands. Many gods were associated with activities in daily life. Families also had their own gods, which took the form of animals, birds, or fish.

The Polynesians told many different **myths** about the creation of the world. Many Polynesians believed that the god Tangaroa *(TAN guh ROH uh)* created the world by separating the earth from the sky. According to some myths, all creatures, including people, emerged from Tangaroa's body. In others, Tangaroa shaped the first people from maggots. According to still other myths, the god Maui *(MOW ee)* created the world by hauling land up from the bottom of an endless ocean with his fishing line.

The Samoans and Tongans worshiped their gods in wooden temples. Other Polynesian peoples worshiped in the open air in walled courtyards called **marae** *(muh RY)*. At one end there was a stone platform called an **ahu** *(AH hoo)*. Prayers called the gods to the ahu. Important gods had full-time priests to attend them. Less important gods had part-time priests. Worshipers chanted and prayed to the gods and performed **rituals**, often with music and dancing. To win their help, worshipers gave the gods sacrifices of food and, sometimes, people.

The Land of the Dead

Polynesians believed that their ancestors came from a mythical land called **Hawaiki** *(ha wa EE kee)*. When people died, their souls returned to Hawaiki. Wrongdoers suffered punishment in Hawaiki, but people who had obeyed the **taboos** enjoyed a happy afterlife, with plenty of eating, singing, and dancing. In societies with powerful chiefs, such as Tonga and Hawaii, it was believed that chiefs would have a better afterlife than commoners. Some great chiefs and priests became gods after they died.

Souls that did not reach Hawaiki became wandering ghosts. Ghosts were good or bad depending on the kind of person they had been when alive. The Polynesians also believed in spirits. These were frightening beings that caused illness and death and fed on souls. They appeared as flashing lights, animals or giant human beings. Sorcerers commanded spirits to harm or kill people they had cursed.

▶ Wood carvings of Hawaiian gods stand on the wall of a Hawaiian marae, or walled compound. Polynesians believed that the carvings contained the **mana** of the gods they represented.

FESTIVALS AND CEREMONIES

Festivals were an important part of Polynesian life. Having a good time was only part of the story, however. Festivals were meant to honor the gods, and they were a chance for chiefs to show off their wealth and rank. **Taboos** outlawed war during festivals.

During festivals, chiefs gave gifts to their people from their storehouses and invited them to feasts. Whether it was at a feast or a religious ceremony, people sat in order of their social rank. People of lower rank got less valuable gifts than those of higher rank and last choice of the food.

The Makahiki

Festivals marked important stages of the year. The Makahiki *(mah kah HEE kee)* festival celebrated the Hawaiian New Year, which came at the end of the harvest season in October or November. The Makahiki lasted for four months and was divided into three stages.

The first stage was a time of **purification.** The chief's tax collectors went around the villages collecting crops, pigs, chickens, dried fish, cloth, mats, and feathers. These things were taken to the local temples and offered to Lono, the god of farming. Priests carried an image of Lono around the island to show the god all the offerings. The second stage of the festival was a time of feasting, singing, dancing, and sports contests. In the final stage, a canoe loaded with offerings was

▼ A modern re-creation of the procession of a Tahitian king. The king wears a cloak of exotic birds' feathers and is being carried on a litter on the shoulders of his subjects.

▲ Participants in a kava ceremony on Samoa drink from a shared cup in order of their social rank. Only chiefs drank from their own cups, which were taboo for commoners to touch.

set adrift on the ocean as a gift for Lono. The festival closed when the chief had a **ritual** fight with a group of warriors to prove that he was still strong enough to rule for another year.

Social Ceremonies

Social ceremonies marked the stages of life from childbirth through adulthood, including marriage and death. Funerals were the most lavish ceremonies and lasted for days or even weeks. Wild behavior was expected at funerals, which included loud wailing, feasting, and dancing. It was important to conduct proper funeral rituals to help dead souls reach **Hawaiki,** the land of the dead.

DRINKING KAVA

Kava *(KAH vuh)* is a stimulating, nonalcoholic drink made from the root of the kava plant, which is related to the pepper plant. Kava has a yellow-green color and a bitter flavor. It was used only in ceremonies marking special occasions, such as a meeting of chiefs, the preparations for battle, or the inauguration of a new chief.

HEALTH AND MEDICINE

Polynesians believed that diseases and illnesses had **supernatural** causes. Disease was thought of as an alien fluid that seeped into the body because the sick person had offended a spirit, broken a **taboo**, or been cursed by a sorcerer.

Polynesians generally enjoyed good health. They did not suffer from many infectious diseases partly because they were so isolated from other peoples. Polynesians also had strict rules for cleanliness, and they washed every day. They plucked any hair from their faces and underarms.

Polynesian healers specialized in different branches of medicine, such as delivering babies, treating children's illnesses, or setting broken bones. Some healers had an expert knowledge of **medicinal** *(muh DIHS uh nuhl)* plants. Others used massage to treat aches and pains. There were even healers who treated mental illnesses. Healers used herbal medicines to treat the symptoms of diseases, but

▲ The noni tree, which bears fruit year-round, was the most important of all the plants used by Polynesian healers to treat people with medical problems.

MAGIC

Polynesians strongly believed in the power of magic to help or harm. People performed magic by chanting charms—for example, when fishing or planting crops—to bring good luck. If they wished to harm someone, people visited a sorcerer. Sorcerers could command spirits to make the victim become ill or die.

Polynesians did not believe that these medicines could cure an illness by themselves. Healers also tried to find out what offense a patient had committed. Only then, they believed, could they cure the illness by performing **rituals** and magic to send the angry spirit away. However, it was believed that if the gods wanted someone to die, there was nothing a healer could do.

Polynesian **myths** tell how plants originally came from the human body. Plants were believed to be linked with the organs from which they formed. This was what made plants useful as medicine. Many common plants had medical uses. **Breadfruit** bark cured headaches, and breadfruit flowers were used to treat ear infections. The stems of the **taro** plant stopped bleeding. **Kava** was used to treat headaches. People suffering from earaches, colds, and lung infections were given turmeric. Arrowroot was mixed with clay to treat diarrhea.

The Amazing Noni Berry

To the Polynesians, the noni tree was the most important of all medicinal plants. Various parts of the tree were used as a cure for boils and sores, coughs, diarrhea, eye infections, fevers, nausea, sore throats, and worms. Noni juice was also used to kill head lice. Noni mixed with kava root, sugar-cane juice, and water was used to treat tuberculosis *(too BUR kyuh LOH sihs)*, a serious lung disease. Noni trees bloom all year round, so the fruit is always available. Unfortunately, noni fruit is known for its unpleasant smell and taste.

Most Polynesian medicines were made by squeezing the juice from a plant's leaves, bark, or fruit and mixing it with water. Polynesian medicines usually tasted unpleasantly bitter. After taking medicine, patients chewed a piece of sweet coconut meat to take away the bad taste.

▶ Polynesians used the roots of the kava plant to make a cure for headaches. Kava was also used to make a stimulating drink used in ceremonies.

POLYNESIAN ART

▲ A carving of human figures from Tahiti probably represents gods or ancestors. Polynesians believed that owning such carvings brought mana to themselves and their households.

Polynesians made beautiful works of art with wood, stone, painted cloth, woven mats, feathers, and flowers. Polynesians did not value fine art just because they thought it was pretty, however. Fine objects were valued because they contained **mana**.

Woodcarvers were the most important Polynesian artists. They carved statues and smaller figures, called **tikis**, of gods and important ancestors. Gods always had a human-like form. Each carving contained the mana of the god or of the ancestor it represented. In the Marquesas Islands and on Easter Island, gods and ancestor figures were sometimes carved in stone.

Statues were placed in temples or at the boundaries of sacred spaces. Temporary houses were built for the statues during religious ceremonies, and the statues were dressed in fine clothes. Priests communicated with the gods and ancestor spirits through the statues. Worshipers offered sacrifices of food to the statues. After the ceremony, worshipers ate the food at a feast. People also owned their own statues of gods and ancestors. People who fished kept small tikis of the sea god Tangaroa *(TAN guh ROH uh)* in their canoes. Before setting out to fish, they made offerings to Tangaroa for a bountiful catch.

Carving was a sacred process. On the island of Mangareva, carvers went through a **purification ritual** before they began work. This brought them under the influence of the gods of woodcarving, Motu-ariki *(MOH too ah ree kee)* and Te Agiagi *(tay AH gee AH gee)*.

Mysterious Petroglyphs

On many islands, Polynesians carved **petroglyphs** *(PEHT ruh glihfz)*. The largest numbers of petroglyphs are found on Tahiti and the Marquesas Islands. Polynesian petroglyphs include geometric designs, human-like figures, and sometimes turtles and fish. The Easter Islanders carved petroglyphs of birdmen. Experts are unsure what these petroglyphs mean.

RONGORONGO

Rongorongo *(RAHN goh RAHN goh)* is a unique form of writing invented by the Easter Islanders. Rongorongo uses picture symbols to stand for words, ideas, or sounds. The symbols were carved onto wooden tablets. The skill of reading rongorongo has been lost, but it is thought that rongorongo was used to record religious chants. The islanders probably got the idea of writing from Spanish sailors who visited in 1770. No other Polynesians used writing before modern times.

▲ Circular petroglyphs on the island of Hawaii may have been carved as part of a ritual to ensure a long life for a newborn baby. Some archaeologists think Hawaiians placed part of the umbilical cord of a newborn in a hole carved in the center of a circular petroglyph. The people believed that if the cord was still there the next day, the child would have a long life.

TATTOOS

Polynesians decorated their bodies with permanent tattoos. They believed that tattoos displayed their **mana**. Some designs were signs of social rank. Tattoos also had protective qualities. People who fished, for example, often had shark tattoos to protect them from real sharks.

Tattooing is an ancient custom that was widespread in Asia and among American Indians and some Africans. Polynesian tattooing was the most skillful in the ancient world. According to Samoan tradition, two women from the island of Fiji introduced the art of tattooing to Polynesia. The word *tattoo* comes from the Polynesian word *tatau*, meaning *the results of tapping*. The word was adopted by British sailors who visited Polynesia in the 1700's. Tattoos became extremely popular with sailors in the 1800's.

How It Was Done

A tattoo is made by pricking the skin with a needle so that dye can be injected under the skin to create a design that would never wash off. Polynesian tattooists made their dye by mixing soot with water. The tattooist dipped a needle made of bone into a dye and repeatedly tapped it into a person's skin using a wooden mallet. For dyeing large areas quickly, the tattooist used a tool with many needle points. Making a complex design took several days or even weeks. Polynesians respected tattooists for their skills and paid them with pigs and other food in exchange for their work.

◀ Elaborate tattoos decorate the body of a Tahitian chief from the Marquesas Islands, in a painting dating from around 1820. On these islands, men covered almost their entire bodies with tattoos. The patterns of Marquesan tattoos symbolized spirits, legendary heroes, plants, animals, feathers, eyes, and even tools.

THE TATTOO HOUSE

In the Marquesas Islands, young men lived in a temporary tattoo house while being tattooed for the first time. The house was **taboo** to women. Drummers outside played gentle rhythms to help the young men endure the pain of tattooing.

Both men and women had tattoos. Tattooing often formed part of adulthood ceremonies. No one was tattooed until he or she had stopped growing. This ensured that the designs would not stretch and lose their beauty. Different islands had different tattoo styles and designs. In Samoa, designs were based on straight lines and right angles. On other islands, curved shapes were used. No two people had exactly the same design.

▲ A modern Tahitian man with traditional tattoos. Tattooing virtually died out in Tahiti in the 1800's because of the influence of Christian **missionaries.** The art was revived in the 1980's, and tattoos have become increasingly popular among Tahitian men.

Tattoos

Men traditionally had more of their body tattooed than women did. In the Marquesas Islands, men tattooed almost their entire body, including their face. Marquesan women tattooed only their hands, arms, stomach, and lower back. Tongues were sometimes tattooed in Hawaii. Being tattooed was painful. It could take a few days to recover from having a large tattoo. Young men proudly displayed their tattoos to show that they could endure a great deal of pain.

ENTERTAINMENT

▲ A large ceremonial drum from Tahiti was carved from a hollowed-out tree trunk. Drums kept the rhythm at dances.

Polynesians enjoyed music, dance, singing, and chanting, and they played many sports. Dancers and other entertainers were highly trained professionals.

Polynesian dances were a way to honor the gods and to praise chiefs and visitors in an exciting and enjoyable way. While they performed, dancers chanted long poems telling stories about gods, **myths**, and heroes. Rhythmic music was played to accompany the dancers. Dancers rehearsed for weeks or months before an important performance. Movements of the eyes, hands, and arms were considered to be the most important in Polynesian dance. Dancers kept time with leg movements.

The most famous Polynesian dance was the Hawaiian hula *(HOO luh)*. Hula dancers made wavy movements with their arms and hips while they were kneeling or standing. Women dancers wore short skirts made of **tapa** *(TAH puh)*; male dancers wore loincloths. Both men and women wore necklaces of flowers.

The Tongan paddle dance was one of the most complicated Polynesian dances. Large groups of men carried painted wooden paddles. The dancers moved the paddles slowly and gracefully as they formed lines, squares, and semicircles. Paddle dances were performed for the king. They symbolized the unity of the people, working together like the crew of a canoe.

Musical Instruments from Nature

Polynesians played a variety of musical instruments to accompany dancers and singers. Large drums made of hollowed-out coconut tree trunks kept the rhythm. Dancers tied small drums made of empty coconut shells covered with fish skin to their legs and beat them as they danced. People made rattles by placing pebbles in a hollowed-out gourd, and they made trumpets out of large seashells. Musicians played bamboo flutes by blowing through their nose, rather than their mouth.

Surfing and Other Sports

Polynesians enjoyed sports. Surfing is the best-known Polynesian sport today, but canoe racing, wrestling, spear throwing, and kite flying were all popular. Hawaiians raced sleds down muddy hillsides. Polynesians played many ball games. Apai *(ah PY)* was a Hawaiian team game similar to lacrosse that was played with wooden clubs. Players tried to drive a ball made of knotted fibers through a bamboo goal. Polynesians also played a game similar to checkers using a stone board and pebbles of white coral and black lava.

▼ Invented by the Hawaiians about 600 years ago, surfing is perhaps the best-known and most popular Polynesian sport. In Hawaii, surfboards were status symbols. Chiefs used boards that were 12 to 18 feet (4 to 6 meters) long. Commoners could use only shorter boards that were about 9 feet (3 meters) long.

SURFING

Polynesian sailors had to be good at getting their boats through heavy surf to land safely on beaches. They made a game out of practicing by using wooden planks to ride the waves into the shore. Separate surf zones were reserved for chiefs and commoners. Hawaiian Duke Kahanamoku *(kah HAHN ah MOH koo)* turned surfing into a worldwide sport after he introduced it to Australia in 1915.

TOOLS AND TOOLMAKING

The Polynesians used simple tools of bone, shell, stone, vegetable fibers, and wood. Important tools possessed **mana** and had to be treated with respect.

The most important tool for woodworking was the **adz**, a hand tool resembling an ax. Adzes were used to chop, shape, and smooth wood. They were especially useful for making planks for building. Adz blades were made from such hard volcanic stones as **basalt** *(buh SAWLT)*. Craftspeople chipped the stone with another stone to shape the blade. They then used a grindstone to finish the blade, making it sharp and polished. Finally, the craftsperson tied the blade to a wooden handle with rope. Adzes made of rare stone became status symbols for chiefs.

Craftspeople made knives and other small tools by striking flakes off a stone using another stone as a hammer. **Obsidian** *(ob SIHD ee uhn)*, a kind of natural volcanic glass, was the best stone for this task. Hard and brittle, obsidian breaks to create razor-sharp edges. Hard woods were also used to make knives and such weapons as spears and clubs.

▲ The long obsidian blade of an adz (facing downward) has been bound tightly to an L-shaped wooden handle, so that it will not slip during use. Only the cutting edge extends beyond the handle, reducing the chance that the adz will break.

Tools from Sea and Land Creatures

Seashells made good tools for scraping and shredding. People used larger, thicker seashells for digging. The Polynesians made fishing hooks of seashells, turtle shells, and animal and human bone. People who fished believed that hooks made from human bone were best because they possessed mana. Bone made good knife blades, spearpoints, and harpoon points. It was also used for drills, needles, and pegs.

No part of an animal was wasted. The front teeth of rats made excellent small chisels for fine woodcarving. Sharkskin, which is rough, was used like sandpaper for smoothing and polishing wooden objects.

The Polynesians abandoned the Lapita custom of making clay pots, partly because the Lapita used up the limited amount of good-quality clay in the Pacific Islands. To carry liquids, Polynesians used wooden bowls or hollowed-out coconut shells. Fibers from bark, leaves, and coconut shells were twisted together to make ropes and fishing lines. People wove ropes into mats, baskets, and fishing nets.

THE STONE TRADE
Good stone for toolmaking was scarce on coral islands. People on these islands relied on long-distance trade to get the high-quality stone tools they needed. An adz that was discovered by **archaeologists** in the Tuamotu **Archipelago** was made of stone found only on the Hawaiian island of Kaho'olawe—2,500 miles (4,000 kilometers) away.

◀ A highly polished adz from New Zealand is made of a rare type of stone called nephrite *(NEHF ryt)*. Tools of this high quality gave mana and status to chiefs and were handed down from one generation to the next. They were used only ceremonially—for example, to begin work on a new house or canoe.

SEAGOING CANOES

Boatbuilding was the Polynesians' greatest technological achievement. Polynesians used narrow **outrigger** canoes for fishing and for journeys to nearby islands. An outrigger is a float attached to a canoe, running parallel to the boat. The outrigger helps to balance the canoe and prevent it from turning over in strong winds and rough seas.

For long journeys on the open ocean, Polynesians used large voyaging canoes. Voyaging canoes were really two large canoes fastened side by side with a platform built on top. Passengers were sheltered from the rain and sun in a cabin built on the platform. There was also a hearth so that voyagers could light cooking fires while traveling. Voyaging canoes were from 50 to 100 feet (15 to 30 meters) long. They had room for more than 100 people and enough supplies to stay at sea for six weeks.

▼ An artist's rendering of a Tahitian **clan** preparing an oceangoing canoe for a voyage to colonize a new island home. Provisions for the voyage, as well as the tools, seeds, and farm animals that the clan would need to found a new settlement will be stored in the two hulls of the canoe. The thatched cabin under construction will shelter the passengers from sun and rain. A clay hearth on the deck near the cabin will even allow for a cooking fire while at sea.

Both types of canoes could be paddled and had one or two masts and sails. Mats made of coconut palm leaves were sewn together to make the sails. Different shaped sails were used on different islands. On Tonga and Hawaii, claw-shaped sails were used. In Tahiti, sails were shaped like half a claw, and in Samoa, they were triangular.

European explorers were impressed by how fast and maneuverable Polynesian boats were. In 1976, the *Hokule'a*, a modern replica of a voyaging canoe, sailed 2,000 miles (3,200 kilometers) from Tahiti to Hawaii in only three weeks.

Look, No Nails!

Both outriggers and voyaging canoes were built in a similar way. A log hollowed out using stone **adzes** formed the bottom of the boat. The boat's sides were made with planks of wood. Boatbuilders shaped the planks with stone adzes. Using drills made of bone, they bored holes along the edges of the planks and the hollowed-out log. Ropes pulled tightly through these holes tied the planks and the bottom of the boat together. Coconut fiber soaked in sticky plant gum was hammered into the cracks between the planks to make the boat watertight. Finally, wooden frames were fastened inside the boat to make it stronger.

▲ A small outrigger canoe is paddled off the coast of Hawaii. Small canoes like this were used for fishing and for short journeys between neighboring islands.

FOOD FOR VOYAGING

The main foods taken on long voyages were fermented **breadfruit** and dried fruit from the pandanus *(pan DAY nuhs)* tree. Wrapped in palm leaves, these foods stayed fresh for months. Coconuts provided food, drink, and fuel for fires to cook fish caught by the crew. Dried shellfish made good emergency rations but were very tough to chew. Water was carried in hollow bamboo stems.

POLYNESIAN NAVIGATION

The Polynesians were the most skillful sailors of ancient times. In a vast ocean, they traveled safely from one tiny island to another. Without the aid of the compass, Polynesian sailors could **navigate** *(NAV uh gayt)* accurately across hundreds of miles of open water.

▶ The red-footed booby can travel up to 30 miles (50 kilometers) out to sea to dive for fish, but returns to land at night. Polynesian navigators watched the flight of the booby for clues about the direction of land.

To navigate, Polynesian sailors relied mainly on the movement of the sun and the stars. They learned the positions of the sun and of the brightest stars and **constellations** *(KON stuh LAY shuhnz)* in the sky at different seasons of the year. This knowledge helped sailors determine the direction of north without a compass. It also allowed sailors to figure out their **latitude** *(LAT uh tood)*, or distance north or south of the equator. To reach an island that was northeast of their starting point, sailors sailed north. Once they reached the same latitude as the island they wanted to go to, the sailors changed direction and sailed east. This course would then take them directly to their destination. Sailors memorized the latitudes of islands they visited or learned them from more experienced sailors.

A Keen Eye for Navigating

Polynesian sailors did not depend entirely on the stars to navigate. Their knowledge of wave patterns, weather conditions, and wildlife also helped them. If clouds covered the sun or stars, sailors could still tell roughly which direction they were sailing in from the general direction of the waves, which varies less than the direction of the wind.

In addition, Polynesian sailors knew that clouds build up over mountainous islands. They were also aware that the color of light reflecting from the sea onto the bottom of clouds provides important information. The color can indicate the position of a low-lying coral **atoll**. Light reflected from the shallow water in an atoll's lagoon is greener and brighter than light reflected from the open sea.

The behavior of birds was another sign used by Polynesian navigators. The flight of birds that feed at sea but roost on land pointed the sailors' way to shore. Using clues like these, skillful navigators were able to detect the presence of land when they were still as far as 60 miles (100 kilometers) out at sea.

CHARTING THE WAVES WITH STICK CHARTS

When waves hit an island, smaller waves are reflected back into the sea. Every island reflects waves in a different pattern. Experienced sailors could recognize which island they were approaching just from the wave pattern. Sailors also made stick charts (below) to teach less experienced sailors how to recognize the patterns. In these charts (which were not actually taken on voyages), the sticks showed the waves, and shells represented islands.

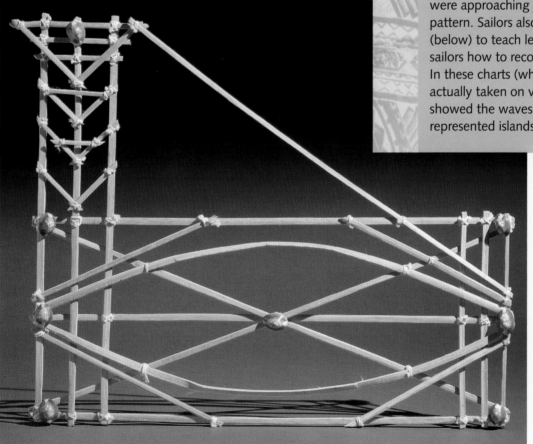

THE FAMILY AND CHILDREN

The extended family was the normal family unit throughout Polynesia. Several generations—grandparents, parents, children, uncles, aunts, and cousins—all lived together, often under one roof. The oldest man was the head of the household.

The birth of a child was always an important event. It was the grandfather's right to announce the birth to the community and the gods. Relatives gave newborn children presents for use in later life. Polynesians were affectionate parents, but they expected their children to be obedient. Parents allowed teenagers plenty of freedom, but young adults had to follow rules and behave responsibly.

▲ A Tongan family plays on the beach. While Polynesians were affectionate parents, their work left little time to enjoy playing with their children.

GROWING OLD

Polynesians gained status with age. Older people were respected for their experience and wisdom but only while they were still active. No one retired in Polynesia. The elderly were expected to do what work they could. Those who became too frail to work were often neglected by their families.

Both parents needed to work, so young children were looked after mainly by their older brothers and sisters and by their grandparents. Adoption was common in Polynesia, and children were given to adoptive parents for various reasons. For example, parents might give a child to another couple who had no children or had no male children. Adopted children treated their adoptive parents in the same way that they would treat their biological parents. Adoption helped create strong bonds between families.

Children did not receive a full-time education unless they were training to be priests. Priests in training took years to learn and memorize tribal traditions and sacred knowledge. Most children learned the skills they would need as adults by working with their parents. Children who wanted to learn a craft became apprentices to experienced craftspeople. Their training lasted several years.

Becoming an Adult

Ceremonies marked the time when a boy or girl became an adult—usually between the ages of 15 and 20. Many adulthood ceremonies involved getting a painful tattoo. Another preparation for adulthood was "fattening." Young girls, in particular, were kept out of the sun, fed large amounts of food, and prevented from taking exercise to make them fatter and paler. Polynesians believed that this made them more attractive and improved their chances of a good marriage.

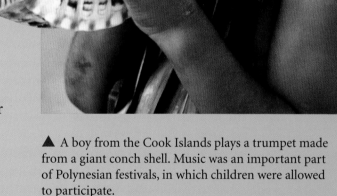

▲ A boy from the Cook Islands plays a trumpet made from a giant conch shell. Music was an important part of Polynesian festivals, in which children were allowed to participate.

Men and women married as soon as they became adults. Marriages were often arranged and always needed parental agreement. Women went to live with their husband's family. **Taboos** forbade marriage to close relations and to people of a different class. If a marriage ended in divorce, the property and children were divided. The older boys went with their father, the girls and infants stayed with the mother.

MAKING A LIVING

Polynesian men and women traditionally did different work. Men were responsible for fishing, building houses and canoes, and making tools. Women prepared food for cooking or preservation, gathered shellfish, wove baskets, and made cloth. Men and women shared the work of growing and harvesting crops.

Most Polynesians made a living by fishing or growing crops. Much of their diet, such as bananas, **breadfruit,** and coconuts, came from trees and did not require a lot of hard work to maintain. **Taro,** a root crop, required the most work to grow. Taro grows best in wet ground. Farmers built soil banks around taro fields to trap water. **Irrigation** channels carried water from streams into the fields. The fields and channels needed constant maintenance and weeding.

Fishers worked from boats or by wading in shallow water near the shore. They used baited hooks and lines, harpoons, and nets. In shallow lagoons, fishers formed a line and splashed the water with stones tied onto the ends of ropes. Fish frightened by the splashing were driven toward long nets and trapped. When enough fish were in the net, it was dragged toward the shore. Fishers then easily speared the trapped fish.

▼ Taro has long been raised for its nutritious roots, which are rich in starch. In Hawaii, taro traditionally has been grown in flooded fields surrounded by earthen banks that trap water.

Families made for themselves most of the things they needed for everyday life. Women wove fibers from coconut and pandanus leaves to make baskets, hats, mats, and ropes. Women also made **tapa** from tree bark for clothes. Men made their own fishing hooks, nets, and digging tools. There were some things commoners could not do for themselves, such as building houses and canoes or making polished stone **adzes**. These tasks were performed by men known as "experts."

The Experts

Experts were men who worked full time in one craft. Smaller communities could support only a few experts, such as a canoebuilder. Larger communities had dozens. In Samoa, experts belonged to **guilds**, which laid down rules and regulations for each craft. There was a total of nearly 30 guilds. The housebuilders', canoebuilders', and tattooists' guilds were the most important. Some of the other guilds were for spear makers, wooden-bowl makers, sailmakers, and stone-toolmakers. Members of guilds were usually related and passed on the secrets of the craft from one generation to the next. Craft skills were passed on in similar ways in other Polynesian communities. Experts were paid for their work with food or other craft products.

▲ A man in the Cook Islands fishes with a spear in the sheltered water of a lagoon. Fishing was traditionally done by men in Polynesian societies.

WEALTH
Polynesians measured their wealth by ownership of such items as tapa, woven mats, canoes, weapons, large houses, and pigs and chickens. Items like seashells and shark teeth were sometimes used as a form of money, but most people simply traded when they needed to buy something.

HOUSES AND VILLAGES

Polynesians lived in small villages. Village life centered on a set of common buildings.

Each family had its own one-room house. Everyone slept on mats on the floor, with their head toward the middle of the house and their feet toward the wall. The most important people in the family slept near the door, and children slept farthest away from the door. The chief's house was the largest house in any Polynesian village. In Hawaii, the chief built his house on higher ground so that it dominated the village. Apart from sleeping mats, Polynesian houses had little furniture. Chiefs owned carved wooden headrests and stools. Lamps burning coconut oil or candlenut oil were lit at night.

EATING APART

It was **taboo** for men and women to eat together in much of Polynesia so villages needed separate eating houses. Men believed that their **mana** was vulnerable when they were eating. Women, therefore, had to be kept away because they might damage or steal a man's mana.

▲ In a traditional Hawaiian house, only the lower parts of the walls were made of stone. Most of the house was made of timber and dried grasses.

◀ A roof made of palm tree leaves tops a typical Tongan house. The walls are made of such modern materials as plywood and corrugated metal. Traditionally, a timber framework thatched with grass was used for the walls.

Besides the houses people lived in, each village had shared buildings used for specific activities. Women wove baskets and mats in the weaving house. Fishers made and stored their nets and fishing hooks in the fishing house. Men and women ate in separate eating houses. Dance and important practical skills were taught in the teaching house. Canoes were stored and repaired in long, narrow canoe houses. There were also storehouses, a guesthouse, and an outdoor cooking area.

Building Materials

The main building materials were wood, dried grass, and woven mats. Stone platforms were used to make firm foundations for important buildings. Carpenters built the framework of a house using timber posts and beams. In Samoan chiefs' houses, posts and beams were carved with elaborate designs. Roofs were thatched with dried grass.

Walls were formed from mats woven from dried grass. Polynesians did not use nails. Ropes were used to lash the timbers together. Different islands had different house designs. Most houses had a simple rectangular shape with a high, steeply pitched roof to shed rain. Warm air rises, so the high roofs also helped keep the houses cool in hot weather.

Grand Plazas

Perhaps the most impressive examples of Polynesian architecture are the tohua *(toh HOO ah)*, or plazas, on the Marquesas Islands. Tohua were raised platforms built of boulders and earth. The chief's house dominated the tohua. Houses for older men, temples, guesthouses, and storehouses were built around the edges of the tohua. The tohua was large enough for all the chief's people to gather for feasts, dances, and religious celebrations.

CLOTHING

◀ Polynesians on a beach on Bora Bora, in the Society Islands of French Polynesia, wear traditional lava-lavas. The light, one-piece garments are well-suited to the tropical climate of Polynesia.

The Pacific Islands have a warm, tropical climate. Polynesians of all ranks wore only simple, light clothing and walked barefoot. Polynesians did not think it was immodest for a woman to show her breasts, but women had to be covered from their waist to their knees. Men sometimes went naked—for example, when fishing or surfing.

Polynesians made clothes from **tapa**, a cloth made from the bark of young paper mulberry trees, and from mats of woven vegetable fibers. Polynesians did not sew cloth. Clothes were made of single sheets of cloth. They were wrapped around the body in different ways to create different styles.

The lava-lava (*LAH vah LAH vah*) was the most common type of clothing in Tonga, Samoa, and Hawaii. Both men and women wore the lava-lava. This was simply a single rectangular piece of cloth that was wrapped around the waist to make a skirt. On Tahiti, women wore a version of the lava-lava called a pareu (*PAHR ay oo or PAH rah oo*). Pareus were brightly painted with flower designs. Women wore the pareu in different ways depending on how warm the weather was. On a cool morning, a woman could wear it as a dress, fastened over her shoulders or under her arms. If the day got hotter, she could wrap it around her waist as a skirt.

Men often wore nothing but a loincloth. This was simply a long piece of cloth that was passed between the legs and fastened around the waist.

Clothing made of woven material was considered less comfortable and was worn only on special occasions. The Tongan ta'ovala *(tah oh vah LAH)* was a colorful formal dress. Tongans traditionally wore the ta'ovala at weddings and funerals. Woven clothes were usually worn over clothes made of tapa.

Fashion Accessories

Men and women wore simple jewelry made of bone, shell, wood, and human hair. Headdresses, necklaces, hairpins, and arm and waist belts were most common. Tongan women wore a kiekie *(KEE ay KEE ay)* around the waist on special occasions. This was a decorative string girdle worn over the top of a lava-lava. Garlands of sweet-smelling flowers were often worn around the neck.

HOW TO MAKE TAPA
Strips of bark from the paper mulberry tree were soaked in water for several days. The rough outer bark was scraped away with a seashell. The inner bark was hammered with a wooden beater until thin and soft. After drying, tapa was dyed or painted with patterns.

▼ An ear bolt from the Marquesas Islands has **tiki** figures carved from a whale's tooth. Such bolts were usually worn by men. Placed through holes made in the earlobes, the bolts could be up to 2 inches (5 centimeters) long.

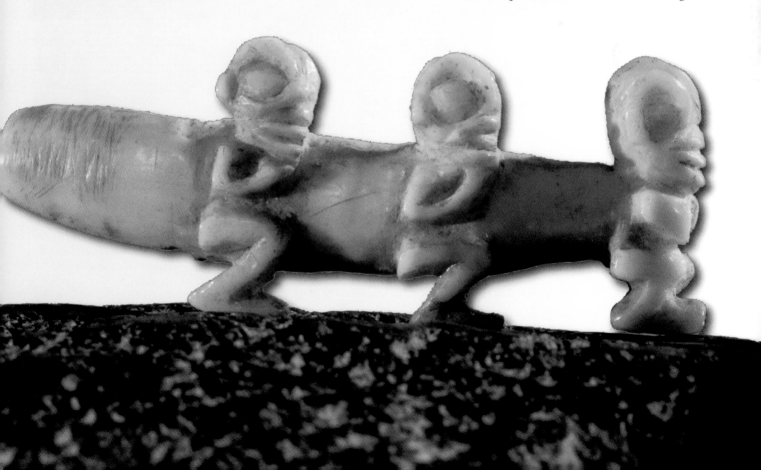

FOOD AND DRINK

Polynesians ate a healthful diet rich in vegetables, fruits, and fish, along with small amounts of meat. Although it was **taboo** for them to eat together, men and women cooked together. People ate with their fingers.

The Polynesians grew food plants that their ancestors had brought with them from Southeast Asia. The two most important foods were **taro** and **breadfruit.** Taro was grown for its thick roots. Taro roots are rich in starch, a good source of energy, but also contain poisons. Cooking taro destroys the poisons. Cooked taro was pounded, mixed with water, and strained to make a bland-tasting blue-gray paste called poi *(poy)*. This was eaten fresh or was buried in a pit and left for a week. During this time, the poi underwent a chemical change, giving it a tangy taste. Breadfruit is the fruit of the breadfruit tree. Like taro, it is rich in starch and bland tasting. It is

▲ Green breadfruit and taro roots were the Polynesians' most important foods. They also ate poi (in bowl), a blue-gray paste made from taro roots that were cooked then pounded and mixed with water.

roasted or baked. Polynesians also ate bananas, coconuts, pandanus fruit, and sweet potatoes. They squeezed the juice from sugar cane and either drank it or used it to sweeten food. They used coconut both for its meat and for its milk. They used few spices but did flavor their food with salt, ground kukui *(koo KOO ee)* nut, and seaweed.

▲ The coral reefs around Polynesian islands provided bountiful supplies of such fish as red snapper and such shellfish as langoustines. Seafood was the main source of protein for most Polynesians.

Besides fish, Polynesians ate such seafood as octopus and shellfish. The fish they found most delicious were skipjack tuna, yellowfin tuna, mahimahi *(MAH hee MAH hee)*, and wahoo *(WAH hoo* or *wah HOO)*. Pork and chicken were the most important meats, but Polynesians also ate dogs and rats.

Slow Food

Polynesians roasted their food or cooked it slowly in simple ovens. The preparation for a big meal began the day before. To make an oven, a hole was dug in the ground. Stones were placed at the bottom of the hole, and a fire was lit. The fire was left to burn overnight to heat the stones white-hot. In the morning, layers of food were placed in the hole on top of mats to protect them from the hot stones. Fruits and vegetables were placed at the bottom, then a whole pig, and then fish. The whole meal was covered with banana leaves and left to cook until evening.

TABOO FOODS

Not all Polynesians could eat what they liked. Some foods were taboo at certain times of the year, when they could not be eaten by anyone. Other foods were taboo to certain people all the time. Hawaiian women, for example, never ate pork, chicken, turtle, or coconut. These foods were taboo for women because the foods were offered as sacrifices to male gods.

EASTER ISLAND

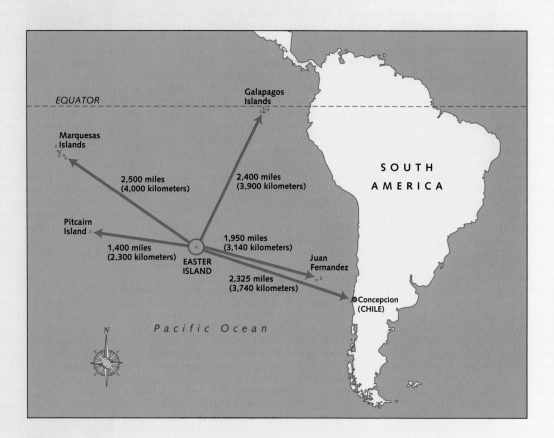

EQUATOR

Galapagos
Islands

Marquesas
Islands

SOUTH
AMERICA

2,500 miles
(4,000 kilometers)

2,400 miles
(3,900 kilometers)

Pitcairn
Island

1,950 miles
(3,140 kilometers)

1,400 miles
(2,300 kilometers)

EASTER
ISLAND

Juan
Fernandez

2,325 miles
(3,740 kilometers)

Concepcion
(CHILE)

Pacific Ocean

N

◀ Easter Island was settled between A.D. 900 and 1200 by Polynesians who journeyed across huge expanses of open water in voyaging canoes from Pacific islands far to the west.

Easter Island is one of the most remote inhabited places in the world. The islanders' nearest neighbors live on Pitcairn Island, 1,400 miles (2,300 kilometers) to the west. Polynesians discovered and settled Easter Island between 1,100 and 800 years ago.

Easter Island is famous for enormous statues called **moai** (*MOH eye*) carved hundreds of years ago. Moai have long sloping noses, deeply sunken eyes, and big chins. The statues stood in rows on top of stone platforms called **ahu.** The sites where the statues were erected were sacred places where **clan** chiefs were buried.

The islanders carved the earliest statues soon after they arrived. By the time the tradition of creating the statues died out hundreds of years later, nearly 1,000 statues had been made. Teams of stone carvers worked on the statues. The carvers began by quarrying a long, rectangular block of rock using stone picks. They then roughly shaped the head and face. The statue was hauled out of the quarry with ropes and levers and set upright for detailing. Then the statue was dragged to the ahu using a wooden sled or wooden rollers.

THIN PEOPLE AND FAT PEOPLE

Easter Island had two social classes, the fat people and the thin people. The fat people were the powerful chiefs and their families. They got the best food and did not have to work hard. The thin people were the commoners. They had to work for the chiefs and give them part of their food.

▼ A row of giant moai statues on Easter Island. The statues stand on a ceremonial platform called an ahu, which contains the graves of clan chiefs. The statues were thought to represent the chiefs' divine ancestors.

An average-sized moai is about 13 feet (4 meters) tall and weighs about 13 tons (12 metric tons). Experiments by modern scientists have shown that it would have taken a team of 20 carvers about a year to make a moai using stone tools. About 40 people were needed to move it. Hundreds more people helped by making rope and producing food for the carvers.

Why Were the Statues Made?

Making and erecting the statues involved all the people in the community and a lot of hard work. Why did they do it?

The statues represent ancient chieftains who were believed to have come from the gods. The statues linked living chiefs to their ancestors and gave them **mana**. At some point, the chiefs decided that bigger statues would give them more mana. They began to compete with one another to make bigger and bigger statues. The biggest statue would have been 70 feet (20 meters) tall, but it was never completed.

ENVIRONMENTAL DISASTER ON EASTER ISLAND

Polynesians sometimes damaged the natural environment by overfishing and overhunting or by cutting down too many trees. The worst example was on Easter Island.

When Polynesians first settled on Easter Island, it was densely forested with palm trees. The trees were a source of nutritious nuts and timber. The tree roots held water in the ground that slowly seeped into streams and springs. Seabirds nested on the island's cliffs and provided meat and eggs. There was good fishing on the reefs around the island, and there was fertile soil for farming. Easter Island's population started small, with a few hundred settlers. By the 1400's, however, between 6,000 and 7,000 people lived on the island. As the population rose, the islanders cleared more and more of the forest to create fields for farming, to get wood for fires, and to build houses and boats.

The Easter Islanders were divided into more than a dozen **clans**, each with its own chief and small territory. Easter Island covers only 64 square miles (166 square kilometers), and only about half the island is suitable for farming. Most people lived close to the sea. The clan chiefs competed peacefully with one another by erecting giant **moai.** The islanders cut down more of the forests to make sleds, levers, rollers, and ropes to move the statues into position. Unfortunately, few young trees grew to replace the ones that had been cut down. Rats, introduced to the island

▼ Abandoned moai statues litter a mountainside on Easter Island. When war broke out between the island's clans, the statues were left near the quarry where they were made.

by the settlers as a food source, ate most of the seeds. The rats also ate the eggs of seabirds. Soon seabirds nested on only a few small offshore rocks.

Disaster Strikes

By the 1600's, no trees remained on Easter Island. Without tree roots to help hold the soil in place, rain began to wash it away. Without tree roots to hold water in the soil and slowly release it, streams and springs dried up, creating water shortages. Crops died, and the people began to starve. Even fishing became difficult. Without trees, the islanders could not build new boats. Nor could they leave to look for a new home. They were trapped.

Wars broke out between the clans, and the great moai were thrown down. According to stories told by the Easter Islanders, cannibalism was common. By the time the first European explorers visited Easter Island in 1722, the population had fallen to only 2,000 people. Chickens had become so valuable that they were sealed up in stone strong rooms at night to keep people from stealing them.

▲ **Petroglyphs** at Orongo, a village and ceremonial center on Easter Island, may represent the Birdman, the victor in an annual swimming contest who would win power and high social status for his clan.

THE BIRDMAN

After the moai were thrown down, the clan chiefs found a new way to compete peacefully. Every year the clans held a swimming race to an offshore rock. The first swimmer to return with a bird's egg became the Birdman. The Birdman's chief had the honor of being the senior chief for the next year. His clan had the sole right to gather seabirds' eggs for that year.

HAWAII

The most complex society in Polynesia developed on the Hawaiian Islands. These volcanic islands have plentiful rainfall and large areas with fertile soil. The Hawaiians built **irrigation** channels to water the fields and improve harvests. They increased their food supply further by building fish ponds along the coast to breed their favorite fish.

Because Hawaiian farmers grew more food than they needed, it was possible for many people to become specialists. Some people became warriors, priests, roof thatchers, builders, stoneworkers, healers, entertainers, clothmakers, boatbuilders, or bird catchers.

Hawaii developed a rigid class system with dozens of ranks. Hawaiians had to remain in the same social class as their parents. The highest class was the *ali'i (ah LEE ee)*, or royal,

KING KAMEHAMEHA I (1758?-1819)

A bronze statue of King Kamehameha, who founded the Kingdom of Hawaii, stands at Hilo Bay on the island of Hawaii. A comet appeared in the sky around the time that Kamehameha was born. Priests prophesized that he would be a great leader and would defeat all his rivals.

Kamehameha's grandfather, King Alapai, ordered that the child be put to death, but he was brought up in secret. From 1782 to 1810, Kamehameha conquered all the Hawaiian islands and created a single kingdom.

▲ The Ahuena Heiau Temple ("The temple of peace and prosperity"), now fully restored, was built on the grounds of King Kamehameha's palace about A.D. 800. The temple, which is considered a holy place, is closed to visitors.

class. This class was divided into kings, first-rank chiefs, and second-rank chiefs. Each of the Hawaiian Islands had its own king. Kings often fought wars with one another. Below the kings were the chiefs, who each owned a section of land extending from the center of the island to the coast. Everyone who lived in that territory owed the chief taxes, which were paid in the form of food, cloth, labor, or crafts. The chiefs in turn owed service to the king.

The next class was the *kahuna (kah HOO nah)*. This class included priests and the specialist workers. Priests were the highest rank of the kahuna; entertainers were the lowest. Most Hawaiians belonged to the *maka'ainana (mah kah EYE nah nah)*, or commoner, class. The commoners farmed or fished, providing food for the kahuna and the chiefs. **Overseers** made sure that the commoners worked hard. The lowest class was the *kauwa (KOW ah)*, or slaves. They often were people who had been captured in wars. Kauwa were often used for human sacrifices.

Oppressive Taboos

The chiefs used severe **taboos** to oppress the commoners. In Hawaii, it was taboo even to touch a chief's shadow. Food that had been touched by the chief's shadow was taboo and could not be eaten. Breaking any taboo, even by accident, was punishable by death. Chiefs were accompanied by executioners, who strangled taboo-breakers on the spot using a special cord. After he united the Hawaiian Islands under his rule in 1810, King Kamehameha abolished taboos and introduced European-style laws and government.

THE COMING OF THE EUROPEANS

▼ The French ships *Astrolabe* and *Zelée* arrive at the Polynesian island of Nuku Hiva in 1840, in an artist's rendering. The crews, commanded by the explorer Jules Sébastien César Dumont d'Urville (1790-1842), spent three years mapping the Pacific Islands.

In 1521, the Portuguese-born explorer Ferdinand Magellan *(muh JEHL uhn)* became the first European to sail across the Pacific Ocean. He and his men nearly died of thirst and starvation because they did not sight a single island until they reached Guam, in the Mariana Islands. The explorers who came after Magellan searched for an unknown continent called *terra australis* (southern land) that they believed lay somewhere in the south Pacific Ocean.

The first European to meet Polynesians was Pedro Fernández de Quiros *(kee ROHS)*, who explored the Tuamotu **Archipelago** in 1605. In the 1700's,

OMAI, THE FIRST POLYNESIAN TO VISIT BRITAIN

Omai, the first Polynesian to visit Great Britain, arrived from Huahine *(hoo ah HEE nay)*, in the Society Islands, on the H.M.S. *Adventure* in 1774. A good-looking young man, Omai became a celebrity and was introduced to King George III. Omai returned home in 1776 with tales about Britain and gifts of wine, kitchenware, muskets, toy soldiers, a horse, and a suit of armor. Omai was an interpreter for Captain James Cook on his last voyage to Hawaii.

Great Britain and France began sending scientific expeditions to make accurate maps of the Pacific. Scientists sailed on these expeditions to study the people, plants, and animals of the Pacific Islands. In three great voyages (from 1768 to 1771, from 1772 to 1775, and from 1776 to 1779), the British explorer James Cook finally proved that there was no undiscovered continent in the south Pacific.

Early meetings between Polynesians and Europeans often ended in violence. Muskets and cannons gave Europeans a great advantage. At first, the Polynesians believed that the pale-skinned Europeans were ghosts or spirits. Once they understood that the Europeans had useful goods, the Polynesians were eager to trade with them. European goods gave their owners **mana**. After months at sea, European sailors needed fresh meat, fruit, and vegetables. In return, they gave the Polynesians iron axes and knives. The Polynesians tried to steal from European sailors, too, causing many arguments. James Cook was killed by Hawaiians in a fight after he tried to take back a boat they had stolen.

New Foods

European explorers gave the Polynesians the seeds of new crops, including papayas and pineapples, and new farm animals to breed, such as goats, cattle, and sheep. This gave the Polynesians a more varied diet. In the late 1700's, European whalers began to operate in the Pacific. The whalers traded with the Polynesians for fresh food. European traders came to buy copra (dried coconut flesh), which was used to make candles and soap. European traders also sold muskets to the Polynesians, leading to an increase in warfare in New Zealand and Hawaii.

◀ The death of British Captain James Cook at Kealakelua Bay, Hawaii, on February 14, 1779, as depicted by British artist George Carter in a 1781 engraving. Cook's head was smashed with a stone as he turned to give orders to his men. Then the Hawaiians stabbed him to death as he lay on the ground. Four other British sailors died in the fight, and many Hawaiians were killed.

THE COLONIAL ERA

In the early 1800's, European influence increased in Polynesia. Whalers set up permanent bases in Tahiti and Hawaii. **Missionaries** arrived to try to convert the Polynesians to Christianity. The Europeans accidentally introduced such diseases as bubonic plague, cholera, leprosy, measles, and syphilis. Thousands of Polynesians died because they had no natural resistance to these diseases. On Hawaii, the population fell from 300,000 in 1778 to only 70,000 in 1853.

The Polynesians initially showed little interest in Christianity. Missionaries first tried to convert the chiefs, hoping that their people would then also become Christian. Some chiefs realized that becoming Christian would win them the support of the powerful Europeans. After the Tongan chief Taufa'ahau (*TOW fah ah HOW*) converted, British missionaries helped him defeat rival chiefs and become king in 1845. Taufa'ahau adopted a new Christian name, George Tupou, and ruled until 1893.

Missionaries persuaded chiefs to abolish traditional laws based on **taboo** and introduce new ones based on the Bible and European laws. The missionaries tried to ban many customs that they did not approve of, such as tattooing. Many Christian Polynesians became missionaries and helped spread Christianity to other islands.

Loss of Independence

In 1840, the British government took possession of New Zealand. In 1842, France took Tahiti, the Tuamotu **Archipelago**, and the Marquesas Islands. These islands became known as French Polynesia. Chile took over Easter Island in 1888. In 1893, American settlers overthrew the Kingdom of Hawaii with the support of the United States government. In 1898, Hawaii became a U.S. possession. The next year, Germany and the United States took over the Samoan Islands. Only Tonga kept its independence, under British protection.

▼ Queen Liliuokalani (*lee LEE oo oh kah LAH nee*), who ruled from 1891 to 1893, was the last monarch of Hawaii. Although popular with her people, Queen Liliuokalani was overthrown in a coup orgnized by American settlers who wanted the United States to annex Hawaii.

Except in New Zealand, where the Maori fought long wars with the British, the Polynesians accepted foreign rule with little fighting.

The foreign rulers built coconut, pineapple, and sugar-cane plantations. Laborers were brought in from other parts of the Pacific and Asia to work on the plantations. In Hawaii and New Zealand, European settlers soon outnumbered the native Polynesians. Polynesian customs survived best where there were few immigrants, as in Samoa and Tonga.

PAUL GAUGUIN (1848-1903)

Paul Gauguin *(goh GAN)* was a French artist who lived and painted in Tahiti for most of his later life, from 1891 until his death. He was looking for paradise, and he saw—and painted—a somewhat idealized place of natural beauty and beautiful people. His *Femmes de Tahiti (Women of Tahiti)* (above) is typical of his painting style during this time, featuring bright colors and flat planes. But Gauguin was also saddened to see the harm Europeans had done to the Polynesians' way of life. "The natives have nothing, nothing at all to do," he wrote, "and think of one thing only, drinking [alcohol]. Day by day the race vanishes, decimated by the European diseases."

THE POLYNESIANS TODAY

Polynesians today face many challenges. The survival of their languages and customs is threatened, and climate change may make some islands uninhabitable.

After World War II (1939-1945), the United Kingdom granted independence to its Polynesian colonies. French Polynesia is now an overseas territory of France; elected representatives from French Polynesia sit in France's National Assembly in Paris. Hawaii became the 50th state of the United States in 1959.

The Polynesians are in danger of losing their native languages. About 140,000 Polynesians lived in Hawaii in the early 2000's, but only about 2,000 of them could speak the native Hawaiian language fluently. In New Zealand, fewer than one-fourth of the Maori speak their native language. Throughout Polynesia, English and French are now the main languages used in government, education, and the important tourist industry.

Environmental Problems

Polynesians also face serious environmental problems. Fish stocks are declining because of overfishing by fleets from Japan, Taiwan, and the United States. Rising sea levels caused by climate change may make many low coral **atolls** uninhabitable. After World War II, the United States, the United Kingdom, and France used Polynesian islands to test nuclear weapons. The long-term effects of the pollution released by these explosions remains unclear.

▶ A beach resort on Moorea in French Polynesia is one of many places of beauty that draw visitors to the Pacific Islands. Tourism is now the major industry on many Polynesian islands.

▲ Samoan men and women perform a traditional dance for tourists. Such performances help Polynesians keep old traditions alive, as well as teach others about their culture.

Despite these problems, the Polynesians are still flourishing. **Archaeologists** on Easter Island have restored about 15 **moai** to their original positions, emphasizing their cultural significance. Pacific cultural festivals bring people from different islands together to share music, dance, and traditional crafts. Polynesians have adopted European and American technology, music, sports, and crafts but have altered them to suit their cultures. The wives of British **missionaries** taught the Polynesians needlework. Now many islanders make dazzling hand-stitched quilts that are prized as works of art. Hawaiian musicians invented their own versions of European musical instruments, such as the ukulele and the steel guitar. In return, some Polynesian customs, like the sport of surfing, have spread to the rest of the world.

POLYNESIAN CRICKET

Polynesians in Tuvalu and in Samoa play kilikiti *(kee lee KEE tee)*. British missionaries taught the islanders to play the game cricket, but the islanders found it a bit dull. They made the game more exciting by using war clubs instead of bats, a hard wooden ball, and teams of up to 50 people.

GLOSSARY

adz A hand tool resembling an ax, used to chop, shape, and smooth wood.

ahu A raised platform at some Polynesian temples.

anthropologist A scientist who studies humanity and human culture.

archaeologist A scientist who studies the remains of past human cultures.

archaeology The scientific study of the remains of past human cultures.

archipelago A group of many islands.

artifact An object or the remains of an object, such as a tool, made by people in the past.

atoll A low, circular coral island with a lagoon in the middle.

Austronesian A group of related languages spoken in Madagascar, Malaysia, Indonesia, and the Pacific Islands, or people who speak Austronesian languages.

basalt A hard, dark volcanic rock.

breadfruit A large, round, starchy fruit grown on many Pacific Islands.

constellation A group of stars, usually having a geometric shape within a definite region of the sky.

clan A group of people who are related through a common ancestor.

DNA A substance that controls the formation, growth, and reproduction of every living cell. The full name for DNA is deoxyribonucleic acid.

excavate To uncover or unearth by digging, especially used of archaeological sites.

gene A part of a cell that determines which characteristics a living thing will inherit from its parents.

guild A union of the people in one trade or craft to keep standards high and to look out for the interests of their trade.

Hawaiki The mythical land from which Polynesians believe their ancestors came.

irrigation Supplying land with water using ditches or other artificial means.

kava A bitter root used to make a stimulating drink used in ceremonies and as medicine.

latitude Distance north or south of the equator, measured in degrees.

mana Supernatural power or influence that flows through objects, persons, or places.

marae An open-air meeting place found in many Polynesian villages.

medicinal Useful as medicine.

migrate To move from one place to another.

missionary A person who works to spread a religion.

moai Giant stone statues found on Easter Island.

monarchy Government by a monarch, such as a king, queen, emperor, or empress.

myth A sacred story.

navigate To sail, manage, or steer a boat on a course or to a destination.

obsidian A natural glass formed when hot lava flows onto the surface of Earth and cools quickly.

outrigger A float attached to seagoing canoes, or the canoe itself.

overseer A person who directs the work of others.

petroglyph A rock carving, usually a picture or symbol.

purification Ceremonial acts intended to spiritually cleanse a person from objectionable acts or characteristics.

refuge Shelter or protection from trouble.

ritual A solemn or important act or ceremony, often religious in nature.

supernatural Above or beyond what is natural.

taboo The system or act of setting things apart as forbidden. The Polynesians have many taboos under which certain things, places, and persons are set apart or prohibited as sacred, unclean, or cursed.

tapa An unwoven cloth of the Pacific Islands, made by soaking and pounding the soft inner bark of the paper mulberry tree.

taro A tropical plant grown for its starchy underground stems.

tiki A carved image of a Polynesian god or ancestor.

ADDITIONAL RESOURCES

Books

Explorers of the South Pacific
by Daniel E. Harmon (Mason Crest, 2003)

*Fishing for Islands: Traditional Boats and
Seafarers of the Pacific*
by John Nicholson (Allen and Unwin, 1999)

Polynesians
by Christine Webster (Weigl, 2004)

Statues of Easter Island
by Lenore Franzen (Creative Education, 2006)

Web Sites

http://pvs.kcc.hawaii.edu

http://www.pbs.org/wgbh/nova/easter

http://www.polynesia.com/explore.html

INDEX

Acknowledgments

Alamy: 32 (Danita Delimont), 44 (Chad Ehlers); **The Art Archive:** 9, 55 (no photographer credited), 43, 58 (Stephanie Colasanti), 49 (Mireille Vautier), 54 (Bibliothèque des Arts Décoratifs Paris/Gianni Dagli Orti), 57 (Musée d'Orsay Paris/Alfredo Dagli Orti); **Bridgeman Art Library:** 26, 30 (British Museum, London), 28 (National Library of Australia, Canberra); **Corbis:** 4 (Bob Krist), 5 (Jose Fuste Raga), 6, 24, 46, 53 (Douglas Peebles), 7 (James L. Amos), 11 (Yann Arthus-Bertrand), 12 (Roger Ressmeyer), 13, 35 (Reuters), 14 (James Davis/Eye Ubiquitous), 15 (Jonathan Blair), 17 (Wolfgang Kaehler), 19, 39 (Anders Ryman), 20, 59 (Earl & Nazima Kowall), 22 (Peter Guttman), 23 (Jack Fields), 27 (George H. H. Huey), 29 (Charles & Josette Lenars), 31 (HO/Reuters), 36 (Kevin Schafer), 38, 47 (Franz-Marc Frei), 40 (Paul Edmondson), 41 (Hervé Hughes/Hemis), 42 (Phil Schermeister), 52 (Macduff Everton), 56 (Bettmann); **The Mariners' Museum, Virginia:** 37; **Photolibrary:** 25; **Werner Forman Archive:** 1, 16 (British Museum, London), 18, 50, 51 (N. J. Saunders), 21, 45 (no photographer credited), 33 (Otago Museum, Dunedin).

Cover image: **Corbis** (Reuters)
Back cover image: **Shutterstock** (Joop Snijder, Jr.)